Playground Games

Co-operative learning for lively children

by Jenny Mosley & Helen Sonnet

pictures by Mark Cripps

Positive Press

How to use this book

It is important to read the games through before playing them with the children. Begin with one of the more simple games which requires children to play as a group but on an individual basis such as 'December!', 'Horses' or 'Let's all be Olympians'. Then, move on to some of the more imaginative games such as 'Mr Motion', 'Fishes in the Caves' or 'A Giant Step'. There are three different game types and these are illustrated with a different symbol.

  – games where children play as individuals within a large group.

  – team games or games with a competitive element.

  – games which require children to take on different characters.

There are also symbols at the top of the page to show whether or not equipment is needed for each game. Most of the games do not require any special equipment. Where equipment is needed, it is listed underneath the symbol. None of the games requires any unusual equipment and everything that is needed will be found easily in a school PE cupboard. Any words or dialogue which are part of the game are shown in large type.

You may wish to demonstrate any unusual movements or those which the children do not understand. Show the children yourself or point out children who are able to perform the movement well. Many of the games include a rhyme for the children to chant. If you're looking for a game where everyone can join in, then choose one of these. Practise the rhyme a few times with the children before starting the game.

It is up to you to decide when a game is over. Some games will naturally run their course but for others you may choose to stop the game and choose different key players or change the style of movement or you may simply see that the children are tired and need a rest.

Playground Games rules...how to play happily together

Each game has its own set of instructions but all of them will help children to develop a range of social skills that are important in the playground and beyond into adult life. One of the key skills that children will learn when playing these games is to listen carefully and follow instructions. Before you start to play any of the games, insist that the children are quiet and emphasise to them that they must listen very carefully to what you are saying and that they must concentrate for the duration of the game.

When choosing children to be key players, be careful not to choose the children who exude confidence and enthusiasm all of the time. Make sure that you involve some of the less confident children who are likely to stand in the background. They may turn out to be star players!

When choosing teams, it's equally important to try to achieve a spread of talent in each team. This will make the games more fair and make it less likely that one team will win everything. It will also motivate the children if they can see that they have a real chance of winning. Where children need to say a rhyme out loud or move in a particular way, have a few practices before you start the game so that all the children know what is required of them.

Printed by: Heron Press, 19-24 White Hays North, West Wilts Trading Estate, Westbury, Wiltshire BA13 4JT

Published in 2004 by: Positive Press Ltd,
28A Gloucester Road, Trowbridge, Wiltshire BA14 OAA

Text copyright© Jenny Mosley & Helen Sonnet
Illustrations copyright© Mark Cripps

ISBN 095454 1162

These playground games provide a wonderful opportunity for the whole class to engage in enjoyable activities together, thereby developing a positive dynamic within the group that promotes team building and a sense of belonging in the children. Sharing enjoyable activities such as games encourages good relationships between adults and children and between children themselves.

The games also have the added benefit of being designed for playing outdoors and are perfect for large spaces. The games are active and fun. There are team games, games for pairs or groups, and individual activities. Some of the games are competitive, while others focus on turn-taking and sharing. The games require children to listen to and follow instructions and to play by set rules – these are useful social skills for them to acquire.

The 'let's pretend' and role play games are ideal for stimulating imagination and creative thinking. Children can even volunteer their own ideas to add further interest or new developments. Group playground games can be used as part of a physical exercise lesson, as a Golden Time treat or just as an excuse to have fun outside of the classroom.

Helen Sonnet

Jenny Mosley
*(Member of the Q.C.A. PE and
School Sports (PESS) Steering Committee)*

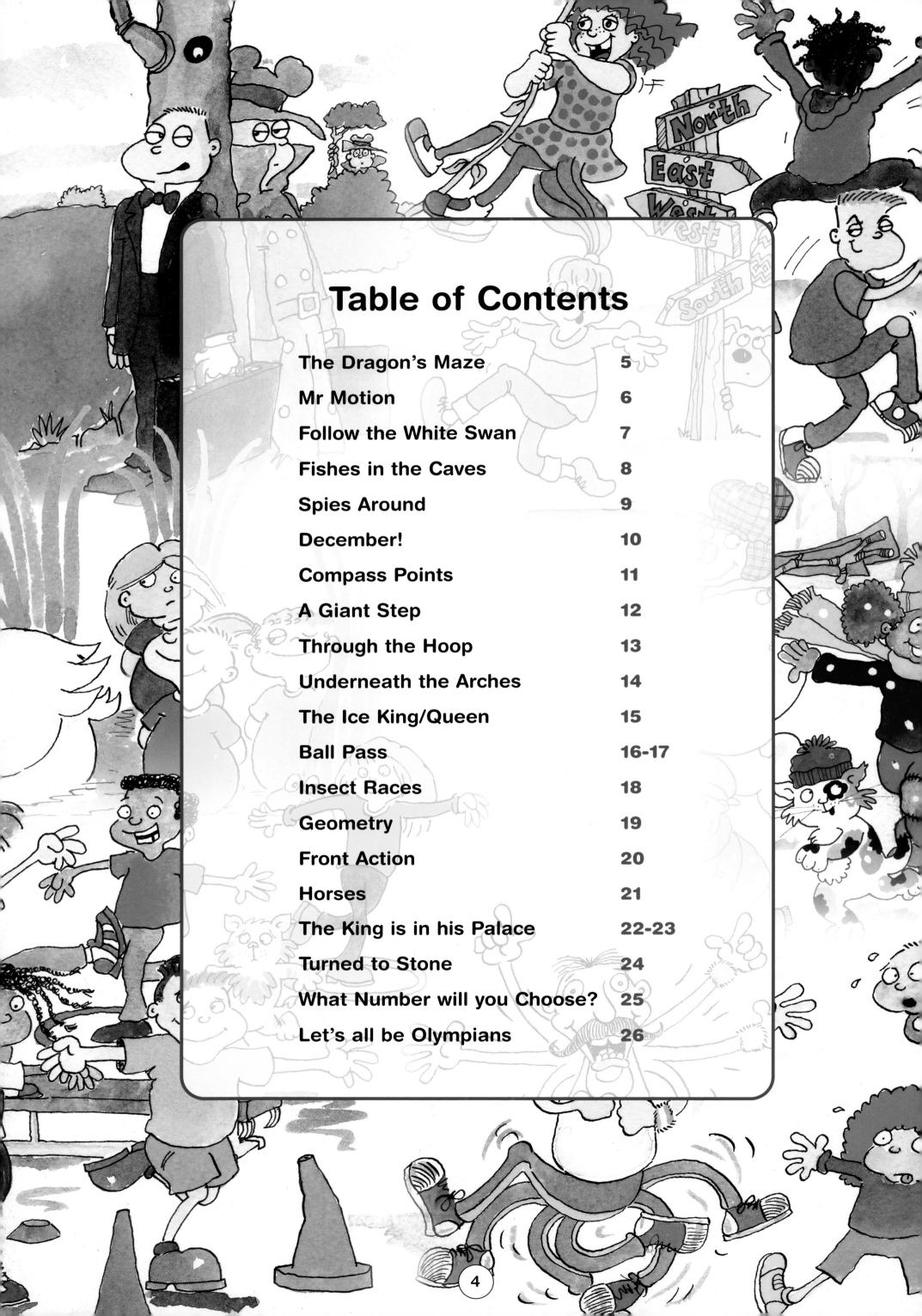

Table of Contents

The Dragon's Maze	5
Mr Motion	6
Follow the White Swan	7
Fishes in the Caves	8
Spies Around	9
December!	10
Compass Points	11
A Giant Step	12
Through the Hoop	13
Underneath the Arches	14
The Ice King/Queen	15
Ball Pass	16-17
Insect Races	18
Geometry	19
Front Action	20
Horses	21
The King is in his Palace	22-23
Turned to Stone	24
What Number will you Choose?	25
Let's all be Olympians	26

The Dragon's Maze

No Equipment

This game requires children to listen carefully and follow instructions.

Choose three children, one to be the dragon, one to be the explorer and one to be the keeper of the maze. Arrange the rest of the children in rows of equal numbers to form a maze. They should all be standing, facing the same way and holding hands along the rows. Any children left over can be additional explorers.

Start the game by telling the explorers to make their way along the passageways of the maze.

Ask the dragon to chase them and try to capture them.

Tell the keeper to shout, **"Turn!"** and stop the game.

On the command of "Turn!", the dragon and the explorers freeze. The children in each row drop hands and make a quarter turn in a clockwise direction to form a new row.

Start the game again.

Each time the keeper calls "Turn!", the children in the rows make a quarter turn to the right to change the direction of the rows. Continue the game until all of the explorers are caught or the children are out of breath. Choose different children to play the parts and begin the game again.

Mr Motion

This game encourages children to use their imaginations and think tactically.

No Equipment

Choose one child to be Mr Motion and ask them to stand in the middle of the playground. Send the rest of the children to one end of the playground and ask them to stand in a line spreading across the playground.

Tell the group to call out the rhyme,

"Mr Motion, Mr Motion, we want to come through, so show us what we have to do."

At this request, Mr Motion describes and shows a way of moving, for example,

"Today I'm having a hopping day."

Encourage the children to hop past Mr Motion to get to the other end of the playground. At the same time, Mr Motion, who is also hopping, tags as many children as he can. Any children who are tagged join Mr Motion in the middle of the playground and help to tag the children trying to pass.

Encourage Mr Motion to choose a different way of moving each time - walking, skipping, crawling, jumping, walking sideways or backwards - and praise imaginative ideas. When all the children have been caught, start the game again with a new Mr or Mrs Motion.

Follow the White Swan

This game will stimulate children's imaginations and encourages everyone to join in.

No Equipment

Choose one child to be the white swan. Ask the remaining children to form a large circle with enough space in between them for others to pass through. Explain to the children that they are going to pretend to be tall reeds by the edge of a pond, and the child playing the white swan will weave in and out among them.

As the game begins, everyone claps and says:

"We'll follow the white swan wherever s/he leads, in and out the water, amongst the tall reeds." "Come," says the white swan, "I'll guide you through the weeds."

As the children say, "Come...", the white swan stops in front of the nearest child and touches him or her on the shoulder.

This child clasps the swan's waist from behind and the two children continue in and out of the reeds as the rhyme is repeated.

Each time the verse is said, another child joins on to the back. Continue until the circle of reeds is too small for the game to be viable.

Fishes in the Caves

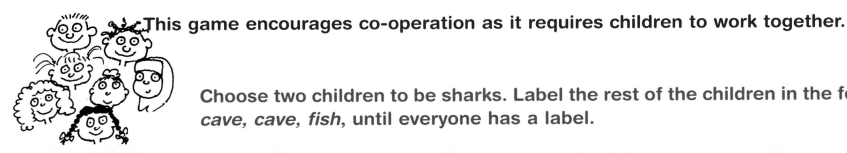

This game encourages co-operation as it requires children to work together.

No Equipment

Choose two children to be sharks. Label the rest of the children in the following order, *cave, cave, fish*, until everyone has a label.

Ask the sharks to stand still in the middle of the playground and tell the caves and fish to move around them.

After a short while, call out,

"The sharks are on the prowl. 5....4....3....2....1."

On your call, each cave has to find another cave. When they have made a pair, ask them to face one another and hold hands. Once two caves have joined together, any fish can swim inside and be safe.

As the countdown reaches 1, the children run. At the same time, the sharks leave their position and catch any caves or fish left floating in the sea. Once caught, they become sharks and the game begins again.

Vary the speed of your countdown to give the sharks or fish a better chance.

Spies Around

Children can use up excess energy by playing this game.

No Equipment

Choose one child to be the spymaster. Organise the rest of the children into pairs. Ask them to form two circles, one inside the other, making sure that one child from each pair is standing directly behind their partner.

Ask the spymaster to stand in the centre of the circle and say,

"I'm looking for a secret agent to be a master spy. I'm going to choose two of you to give it a try."

The spymaster then walks around the inside of the circle, pointing to each pair in turn saying,

"Not you, not you, not you, (until) it's you!"

When the spymaster has chosen a pair, tell the child from the inner circle to run around the outside of the circle in an anti-clockwise direction and the child from the outer circle to run around the outside of the circle in a clockwise direction.

The first child to arrive back at their place, enter the circle and touch the spymaster, becomes the new spymaster. The second child returns to their place and the original spymaster takes the vacant place in the circle and waits for the game to start again.

December!

This game will help younger children to learn the months of the year.

No Equipment

Ask the children to stand in a circle. Choose one child to stand in the centre and be the calendar.

Challenge the children to move around, walking as near to the child chosen to be the calendar as they dare, asking,

"Calendar, calendar what's the month?"

Tell the calendar to choose any month and call it out. The game continues until they choose December.

When the calendar calls **"December!"**, the children turn and run towards the edges of the playground while the calendar tags as many children as they can.

Tell any children who are tagged that they are now helpers and must join in the catching next time the calendar calls "December".

Continue the game until all the children are caught and then choose a new child to be the calendar.

Compass Points

This game can be used as a fun way to learn or revise the four points of a compass.

Choose four places in the playground to represent the four points of a compass.

Tell the children to mingle in the centre of the playground and wait for you to call out a way of moving and a compass point.

These could be: *skip to the South, hop to the East, bunny-jump to the West or walk backwards to the North.*

Explain to the children that they must move in the direction you have called, using the method you have chosen.

The first child to arrive at the compass point gives the next command.

Talk through the various modes of movement with the children before you play the game.

A Giant Step

This game encourages children to think creatively.

No Equipment

Choose a child to be the caller and ask them to stand facing one of the playground walls or sides. Walk with the rest of the children to the opposite end of the playground and give them names - red, blue, green or yellow.

Explain to the children that the aim of the game is to move towards the opposite wall until one of them is near enough to touch the caller.

Begin the game. Ask the caller to name a colour, a number of steps and a way of moving. They shout out commands for each colour, using a different way of moving each time - *Blues take one giant step, Reds take three mouse steps, Greens take two bunny jumps, Yellows take one worm's length.*

The first child to reach the other end of the playground and touch the caller takes on the role of the caller and the game begins again.

To work out a worm's length, the children should lie down and then move to the spot on the ground where their head was. Encourage the children to suggest ways of moving and practise them together so that everyone is clear about the rules of the game.

Through the Hoop

This game fosters co-operation and encourages turn-taking.

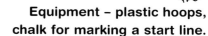

Equipment – plastic hoops, chalk for marking a start line.

Divide the class into two teams of equal numbers. Mark out or use an existing line across the playground as the start line. Ask the children in each team to line up, one behind the other, behind the start line.

Give the first child from each team a plastic hoop and ask them to hold it upright, directly above the start line.

Shout, **"Go!"**   On this command, the team members follow each other through the hoop, held by the first child from each team, and run back to their starting positions.

Once all members of a team are back, tell the next child in the team to take the hoop and the original child joins the back of their team.

Continue the game with each child taking a turn at holding the hoop for their team to pass through.

The first team to have their original hoop holder back at the front of the line is the winner.

Underneath the Arches

This game requires children to work together and take turns.

No Equipment

Divide the class into two teams. Ask each team to stand in a circle. Tell the children in each team to hold hands around the circle and raise their arms to form arches. Remind them to leave sufficient space between them for other children to pass through.

Start the game by choosing one child from each team to pass under the arches, weaving in and out of the circle.

When they arrive back at their original place, ask them to rejoin the circle and the next child repeats the process.

Continue until all the children have had a turn.

The winning team is the first one to have all players complete a circuit of the arches.

The Ice King/Queen

This game encourages tactical thinking as well as thinking of others.

No Equipment

Choose one child to play the ice king if the group is small, or two children to play the ice king and queen if the group is large. You will also need to choose six children to be the captives.

Tell the six captives to stand in a tight huddle and ask the ice king/queen to guard them. The remaining children form a circle around them.

Begin the game by challenging the children to free the captives by touching them. Explain to them that if they are tagged by the ice king/queen, they must freeze on the spot.

Remind the children that they can only free one captive at a time. One child cannot touch all six captives and free them at the same attempt!

Play the game until all the captives are released, all the rescuers are frozen or you decide to let the children swap roles.

Ball Pass

This game encourages turn-taking and sharing.

Ask the children to stand in a large circle.
Start the game by introducing a large beach ball to the group.

Explain to the children that you are going to call out a variety of commands to control the way in which the ball is passed from child to child and the direction it travels in.

Once you have started play, remind the children to listen carefully and concentrate.

At regular intervals, call out these commands in a random order to change the action and direction of the game:

In front - the children stand in an inward-facing circle and pass the ball in front of them.

Behind - the children stand in an inward-facing circle and pass the ball behind their backs.

Through the legs - the children make a quarter turn to the left and pass the ball through their legs.

Over the head - from an inward-facing position, the children make a quarter turn to the left and pass the ball backwards over their heads.

Throw - the children widen the circle by spreading out and throw the ball around the circle.

Bounce - the children pass the ball to the child on their right by bouncing it on the ground for them to catch.

Kick - the children pass the ball gently with their feet.

All change - the children immediately change the direction in which the ball is travelling around the circle. If the children are passing the ball through their legs or over their heads, they will also have to turn and face in the opposite direction.

Insect Races

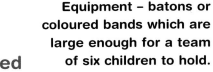

This game fosters co-operation and stimulates imaginative thinking.

Organise the children into groups of six.
Before you start the game, give each group a baton or coloured band that is big enough for all six team members to hold.

Equipment – batons or coloured bands which are large enough for a team of six children to hold.

Explain to the children that they are going to pretend to be insects. As all insects have six legs, each child will represent one leg and will have to move by hopping or jumping with their feet together.

The rule of the game is that all team members must hold the band with one hand, while running the race.

Once the children have chosen their way of moving, let them practise moving together as a group.

Then, hold an insect race over a short distance.

Put the children into new groups and repeat the process.

Each time the children are put into groups, they should choose which insect they are going to be. Encourage them to give their team an imaginative name - *battling beetle, lightning ladybird, whizzing wasp, busy bee, darting dragonfly.*

Geometry

This game encourages quick thinking and co-operative play.

Ask the children to stand together at one end of the playground and wait for your instructions. Explain to them that you are going to call out a variety of cue words. Each cue word requires a different number of children to get together and run to the other end of the playground and back.

Introduce the cue words to the children and have a few practices before starting the game.

Points - all of the children run independently to the other end of the playground and back.

Lines - the children find a partner to run with.

Triangles - three children join up and run together.

Squares - the children assemble in fours to run the course.

Stars - five children group together and run the length of the playground and back.

Hexagons - the children run together in sixes.

Front Action

This game encourages children to follow instructions and play co-operatively.

Equipment - benches, ropes, balls, skittles to make an obstacle course.

Set up an obstacle course for this game to add interest and provide a greater challenge.

Tell the children to form a long line, standing one behind the other.

Ask the child at the front of the line to choose the style of movement - hopping, skipping, crawling, jumping sideways, walking. Encourage them to add simple hand actions - clapping, raising and lowering arms, swinging arms.

The children behind copy the actions of the leading child.

At regular intervals, call, **"Change!"** Then, the leading child goes to the back of the line and the next child steps up as leader.

Each time there is a new leader, encourage them to change the actions.

If there is an obstacle course, the children can lead each other around, under or over the obstacles, while moving in a particular way at the same time.

Horses

This game encourages children to use their imaginations.

Equipment – ropes and skittles.

Explain to the children that they are going to be horses.

Explore and practise the different ways in which horses move. Start with simple movements such as walking, trotting (the children can mimic this by running slowly) and cantering (the children run at a medium pace, leading with one leg).

When they are cantering, instruct the horses to take a jump.

Gradually introduce more complex movements. The children could mime dressage by moving very carefully and taking even paces. They should also have straight backs and pointed toes.

Explore cross-country horse riding which involves fast galloping and jumping fences, going carefully down steep banks and taking water jumps.

For show jumping, place skipping ropes on the floor to represent the jumps on a course.

Challenge the children to be carriage horses. To do this, they should work in pairs and stand side by side, holding each other's hands in front of them. They must step together and practise various paces.

Once the children are skilled at this, try having two pairs of carriage horses, one behind the other and see how well they can match paces. Use a line of skittles for the carriage horses to weave through.

The King is in his Palace

This game is perfect for calming down lively children.

Ask the children to form a large circle.
Choose a boy to be king and tell him to stand in the centre of the circle.

All the children chant:

**"The king is in his palace, palace, palace.
The king is in his palace, he wants to choose a queen."**

Ask the king to choose a queen from the circle of children and, once chosen, she joins him in the centre. All the children then chant:

**"The queen needs a helper, helper, helper.
The queen needs a helper, she wants to choose a maid."**

The queen chooses a maid to come into the centre. All the children chant:

No Equipment

"The maid is feeling hungry, hungry, hungry.
The maid is feeling hungry, she wants to choose a cook."

The maid chooses a cook to come into the centre. All the children chant:

"The cook is feeling nervous, nervous, nervous.
The cook is feeling nervous, s/he wants to choose a guard."

The cook chooses a guard to come into the centre. All the children chant:

"The guard looks after everyone, everyone, everyone.
The guard looks after everyone, and keeps them safe and sound."

During each verse, ask the children in the circle to join hands and walk round. For the last verse, the children in the centre form their own circle and walk round as well.

Turned to Stone

This game will help children to use up excess energy.

No Equipment

Choose two children to play wizards and three more to be elves. Ask the rest of the children to spread out.

Explain to the children that the wizards can cast a spell on them by tagging them. Any child touched by a wizard is turned to stone and must stand still.

Tell the elves that they can reverse this spell by touching the children who have turned to stone.

Only the elves have this power but they must watch out because they can also be turned to stone by the wizards.

Play the game for several minutes, then choose different children to be the wizards and the elves.

24

What Number will you Choose?

This game encourages children to listen to and follow instructions.

No Equipment

Choose one child to be the caller and give each of the remaining children a number from 1 to 6.

Ask the caller to stand at one end of the playground, with the remaining children standing just in front of him or her. The numbered children call out:

"What number will you choose?
Tell us now, tell us now.
We're waiting to hear.
Tell us now, tell us now!
Is it number 1?
Is it number 2?
Is it number 3?"

For each number, ask the caller to answer either yes or no. If the answer is yes, all the children with that number run to the other end of the playground and back again.

The last child to arrive back becomes the new caller and the old caller takes over that child's number.

Choose a new caller and start the game again.

25

Let's all be Olympians

This game requires children to think imaginatively and encourages them to introduce new ideas.

No Equipment

Using the space of the playground, ask the children to pretend to be different Olympians as you call out the various roles.

By miming the actions, they can pretend to be sprinters, high jumpers, hurdlers, long jumpers, triple jumpers, walkers, javelin or discus throwers and so on.

Challenge the children to suggest any other sports from the Olympic Games and discuss the appropriate actions for each one.

Other titles in the Learning Through Action series

Skipping Games

By Jenny Mosley and Helen Sonnet, illustrated by Mark Cripps

The skipping activities in this book are designed to proceed from the simple to truly impressive displays of magnificent agility. They have catchy chants that bring rhythm, humour, exercise, accomplishment and companionship to your playground, making it a happy place full of those who spend their free time doing something that has been enjoyed since rope was invented. You will find both traditional and modern chants in this book. You could even create some of your own.

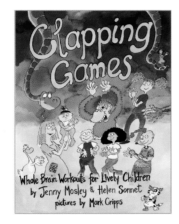

Clapping Games

By Jenny Mosley and Helen Sonnet, illustrated by Mark Cripps

This first collection of clapping games includes old favourites and brand new rhymes. With colourful illustrations and beautiful details, the games in this large format, full-colour book develop listening skills, head and hand coordination, memory and language skills in a fun and entertaining format. Includes CD.

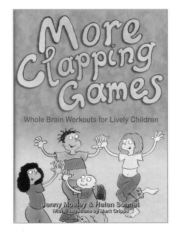

More Clapping Games

By Jenny Mosley and Helen Sonnet, illustrated by Mark Cripps

Building on the success of the first book, this collection (in black and white A4 format) expands the repertoire with 30 new clapping games which will appeal to older as well as younger children. Includes a DVD, demonstrating the games as performed by KS1 and KS2 children.

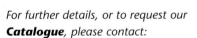

For further details, or to request our **Catalogue**, *please contact:*

Positive Press Ltd.
28A Gloucester Rd
Trowbridge, Wiltshire
BA14 0AA
Tel: 01225 719204
Email: positivepress@jennymosley.co.uk
Website: www.circle-time.co.uk.